My First Space Books

Our Sun Is a Star

Francis Spencer

TABLE OF CONTENTS

A Crabtree Seedlings Book

CRABTREE
Publishing Company
www.crabtreebooks.com

Sun

Our Sun

Our Sun is a **star**.

It **rises** in the sky
every morning.

The Sun is millions of miles from **Earth**, but its light is **powerful**.

Sun

The Sun's light warms Earth's land and water.

The Sun's light helps us see in the **daytime**.

We use sunlight to make **solar energy**.

Light
Energy
Water

Plants need sunlight to make their food.

Many plants are food for people and animals.

Without the Sun, there would be no life on Earth.

Glossary

daytime (DAY-time): Daytime is the time between morning and evening when it is light outside.

Earth (URTH): Earth is the planet on which we live. It is the third planet from the Sun.

powerful (POW-ur-ful): Powerful means having great power or strength.

rises (RIZE-IZ): When something rises, it moves upward.

solar energy (SOH-lur EN-ur-jee): Solar energy is energy from the Sun. It can be used for heating and making electricity.

star (STAR): A star is a ball of burning gases in space.

Index

School-to-Home Support for Caregivers and Teachers

This book helps children grow by letting them practice reading. Here are a few guiding questions to help the reader build his or her comprehension skills. Possible answers appear here in red.

Before Reading

- **What do I think this book is about?** I think this book is about our Sun. I think this book is about the benefits of the Sun.
- **What do I want to learn about this topic?** I want to learn more about how the Sun was formed. I want to learn why the Sun gives off heat.

During Reading

- **I wonder why...** I wonder why the Sun is called a star. I wonder why sunlight is used to make solar energy.
- **What have I learned so far?** I have learned that the Sun's light helps us to see in the daytime. I have learned that the Sun's light warms the land and water on Earth.

After Reading

- **What details did I learn about this topic?** I have learned that plants need sunlight to make their food. I have learned that the Sun is a star of burning gases in space.
- **Read the book again and look for the glossary words.** I see the word *daytime* on page 10, and the words *solar energy* on page 13. The other glossary words are found on pages 22 and 23.

Library and Archives Canada Cataloguing in Publication

Available at the Library and Archives Canada

Library of Congress Cataloging-in-Publication Data

Available at the Library of Congress

Crabtree Publishing Company

www.crabtreebooks.com 1–800–387–7650

Print book version produced jointly with Blue Door Education in 2023

Written by: Francis Spencer

Print coordinator: Katherine Berti

Printed in the U.S.A./072022/CG20220201

PHOTO CREDITS:

Cover, title page and and page 4-5 © Bill Ferngren, page 2-3 ©Aphelleon; cover; page 6-7 © nexus 7; page 8-9 © givaga; page 10-11 ©Tatyana Vyc; page 12-13 © BOONJAEM; page 14-15 ©Paper Teo; page 16 girl ©karelnoppe; page 17 rabbit © Paul Reeves Photography, page 18-19 ©ON-Photography Germany, Page 20: (kids) Hurst Photo . page 20-21 and page 23 © robert_s. All images from www.Shutterstock.com

Published in the United States
Crabtree Publishing
347 Fifth Ave.
Suite 1402-145
New York, NY 10016

Published in Canada
Crabtree Publishing
616 Welland Ave.
St. Catharines, Ontario
L2M 5V6